PHONETICS - I

The Arab grammarians studied the sounds of Arabic in a very systematic (scientific) way. Their main purpose was to preserve the correct pronunciation of the Quran (Qoran, Koran) and to prevent it from any mispronunciation. They described the sounds and also gave detailed descriptions of the organs of speech. As early as in the beginning of the 4th century B.C. the grammarians of Greece and China studied the sounds of their respective languages. Before them an Indian grammarian named Panini also studied the sounds of Sanskrit (c. 5th century B.C.) at the University of Taxila. He is said to be the first phonetician. Their descriptions are very much like what we study today in general phonetics.

Phonetics studies the speech (or **human**, because animal sounds cannot be called so although their sounds may have certain meanings) sounds of the languages of the world. Phonetics is divided into three branches on the basis of the three stages of speech production (articulation), transmission and reception, which is known as the *speech chain*.

Articulatory $\rightarrow$

Acoustic $\rightarrow$ **Auditory**

1. **ARTICULATORY PHONETICS** : This branch deals with the physiological stage of speech production. The speaker's speech organs move in a specific way for every sound. This stage of phonetics studies these movements. It shows how each sound is articulated (produced).

2. **ACOUSTIC PHONETICS** : This branch deals with the physical stage of speech transmission. The acoustic stage follows the articulatory stage. The sounds produced by the speaker disturb the air and cause sound waves like the waves of water in a lake or a sea. Every speech sound has a different sound wave from the other. This stage of phonetics studies these sound waves. It examines them and gives their characteristics.

3. **AUDITORY PHONETICS** : This branch studies the physiological stage of speech reception. The hearer's auditory organs receive sound waves which travel

through the sensory nerves to the brain and the brain understands the sound waves as the sounds of the language (linguistic form). This stage is difficult to understand because some parts of this system are still a mystery to science.

For our study articulatory phonetics is the most important. Therefore, we shall study how speech sounds are produced.

In speech production more than half of our body is needed and used. Different organs of our body come into action while producing speech sounds. The lungs, the muscles of the chest, the larynx, the lips, the mouth, etc. are used to produce speech sounds. These organs are called the ***organs of speech.***

The expression (term) "**organs of speech**" is not very suitable because all these organs are not used primarily for speech. They have functions other than the production of speech. The lungs are necessary for breathing, the teeth are used for chewing food, the tongue is needed for the difference in tastes, etc. But for want of a better expression, the phoneticians continue to call them the ***organs of speech***.

These organs of speech are divided into three groups according to their functions :-

1. **THE RESPIRATORY SYSTEM** : This includes the lungs, the chest muscles, the windpipe (or ***trachea***), the pharynx, and the nose.

2. **THE PHONATORY SYSTEM** : This comprises the larynx and the vocal folds (or ***cords***) inside it. The vocal folds are the sound source.

3. **THE ARICULATORY SYSTYEM** : This consists of the lips, the teeth, the roof of the mouth, the tongue, the pharynx, and the nose.

The ear, too, is very important for speech production. The speaker is also the listener to his own speech. He hears and controls his own sounds while he pronounces them. People who become deaf due to some disease or accident cannot hear their own speech. Therefore, they slowly lose the ability to speak and at last become dumb as well as deaf.

Thus, hearing ourselves is also important as we speak. In phonetics, we call this the *"feedback link"*. It means that the speaker's speech again enters his own ears and helps him to check, control and correct his mistakes.

PHONETICS – II

There is a total number of 44 speech sounds (phonemes) in the **R.P.** (i.e. Received Pronunciation). R.P. is also known as the **B.B.C. English** or **Queen's English.** It is the variety of English spoken by the educated British speakers.

Out of these 44 speech sounds, 20 are vowels and 24 are consonants. A vowel sound is produced orally (not nasally) without any stricture, i.e. closure or partial closure. There is a free flow of air-stream from the lungs.

A consonant sound is articulated with some kind of stricture (closure) in the path of the air-stream. It is easier to explain how a consonant is produced. Phoneticians give three-term labels to both vowels and consonants. These labels are very convenient to learn. On the basis of these three-term labels we can easily describe how a speech sound is produced.

A consonant is studied on the basis of the following three criteria (singular "criterion") :-

(1) Place of Articulation, i.e. from which place the consonant is articulated

(2) Manner of Articulation, i.e. the type of the stricture used to articulate a specific consonant

(3) Position of Vocal Cords (or **Folds),** i.e. whether they are held apart or brought closer.

We can take these reference points one by one and see how consonants differ from one another in relation to each one of them. Further, it is important to understand that the speech sounds can have three positions in a word :-

(i)initial, i.e. in the beginning

(ii)   medial, i.e. in a position when it has some sound(s) before and also some sound(s) after it

(iii)   terminal, i.e. at the end.

Therefore, we shall try to find examples of words where the specific sound occurs initially, medially and terminally. We need to keep in mind that some speech sounds may not occur in all the three positions, e.g. no word in English ends with /h/ or no word begins with / /.

(A) PLACE OF ARTICULATION :-

(a) Bilabial (from/with two lips), i.e. the consonant is produced with two lips

/**p**/   pack, pray, play, pull, part

happy, simple, spray, April, apart

hope, tap, wrap, keep, stop

Note : 1. Remember that this sound is not there in Arabic. Therefore, you will have to work hard to acquire this sound.

2. There is no system of making the same consonant double in a word in English.

Whenever there are two consonant letters together, the first one becomes silent, e.g. the first "p" in "happy".

3. Spellings in English are tricky. It is because 44 speech sounds are handled with only 26 letters of the alphabet. Also, English has borrowed many words from different languages. Notice that **"w"** in the beginning of "wrap" is silent.

/b/   back, buy, beast, because, best

labour, above, cubs, symbol, habit

tribe, rib, robe, club, job

/m/   man, mother, miss, much, most

games, lamp, image, America, among

lamb, room, game, him, team

/w/   where, want, within, watch, wait

sweet, swim, twelve, quite, quick

Note : 1. The sound /w/ cannot come at the end of a word in English.

2. The lips are rounded to produce /w/.

(b) Labio-dental (lip and teeth), i.e. the consonant is produced with the lower lip and the two front teeth.

/**f**/   fast, feel, fan, few, fail

afraid, difficult, office, before, often

cough, off, rough, life, laugh

/**v**/   very, veil, voice, view, value

over, river, seven, travel, heavy

of, twelve, move, believe, have

Note : The sound /v/ is not there in Arabic. Therefore, practise it carefully.

(c) Dental (from/with teeth), i.e. the consonant is produced with the tip of the tongue and the two front upper teeth.

/ /   thick, three, thought, thirty, thirst

author, nothing, healthy, earthy, monthly

faith, fourth, month, south, death

/ /   that, those, their, though, than

either, clothes, breathing, further, worthy

Bathe, smooth, clothe, breathe, loathe

(d) Alveolar (from with the teeth-ridge), i.e. the consonant is articulated with the tip **&/or** blade of the tongue against the alveolar ridge.

/t/   two, town, Tuesday, talk, time

city, better, hotel, notice, watery

eight, but, great, missed, laughed

/d/   down, die, done, dinner, December

idea, Monday, medicine, under, ready

afraid, bad, friend, read, side

/n/   nice, notice, neither, need, know

many, winter, finish, final, enough

green, join, rain, thirteen, begin

/s/   sink, said, south, sleep, start

beside, last, feast, listen,
message

face, cats, piece, advice, pass

/z/   zoo, Zed, zero, zinc, zone

lazy, busy, reason, noisy, losing,
miser

cause, noise, please, breeze, dogs

/l/   leaf, like, loud, learn, late

fellow, allow, foolish, believe,
feeling

tool, mile, fool, ball, owl

Note : The sounds /t/ and /d/ do not exist
in Arabic. Therefore, practise them well.

(e) Palato-alveolar (from/with hard
palate and alveolar ridge), i.e. the
consonant is articulated with the tip of the
tongue at the back of the alveolar ridge
close to the hard palate. (Some
phoneticians prefer to call them "post-
alveolar" consonants.)

/ /   shine, sure, should, sugar, sharp

machine, patient, nation, ashamed, anxious, ocean

push, selfish, punish, wash, fresh

/ /   It does not begin at the beginning of English words.

treasure, decision, pleasure, television, occasion

garage, rouge, beige, barrage

/ /   change, chain, cheap, choice, child

teaching, kitchen, question, future, fortune

March, speech, stretch, which, touch

/ /   joke, July, joy, journey, gentle

danger, soldier, subject, imagine, major

large, message, arrange, bridge, page

/r/   read, round, write, rain, wrong

agree, cross, direct, foreign,

great

It does not occur at the end of
English words in R.P. except when the
following word begins with a vowel (e.g.
"never again'). Then it is called the
linking /**r**/.

Note : The sounds / / and / / are not
there in Arabic. Therefore, make enough
practice to produce them correctly.

(f) Palatal (from/with hard palate), i.e.
the consonant is produced with the tip and
blade of the tongue against the hard palate
as in /**i:**/ or / /.

/**j**/   yes, your, yellow, Europe, use

amuse, failure, few, knew, music

It does not occur at the end of
English words.

(g) Velar (from/with velum or soft
palate), i.e. the consonant is articulated
with the back of the tongue and the soft
palate.

/**k**/   class, kind, cool, kill, country

because, box, breakfast, pocket, school

lock, mistake, music, neck, break

/ /   gave, guard, garden, guess, green

ago, angry, August, forget, regular

bag, plug, drug, leg, dig

/ /   It does not occur at the beginning of words in English.

singer, hungry, amongst, language, hanging

young, sing, wrong, spring, evening

(h) Glottal (from/with glottis) i.e. the consonant is produced from the opening between the vocal cords.

/**h**/   heart, heat, haste, whose, how

Behind, anyhow, key-hole, inhale, greenhouse

It does not occur at the end of English words.

PHONETICS - III

--

(B) MANNER OF ARTICULATION :

The manner of articulation refers to the stricture involved in the articulation of different consonants. The term *'stricture'* means the way in which the passage of air is restricted by the various organs of speech. It is achieved through two processes :-

(i) **"Oro-Nasal Process"** or **"Position of the Velum"** :- Speech sounds can be classified as *'oral'* or *'nasal'*. This depends upon the position of the velum or soft-palate. If the soft palate (velum) is raised, it makes a firm contact with the back wall of the pharynx and shuts off the nasal passage and allows the air to pass through the oral passage. This is called **velic closure**.

All the 20 vowels in English R.P. are articulated through the oral passage. Therefore, all the vowels are oral. In some languages, like French and Hindi, there are nasalized vowels which are produced by allowing the air to pass through both the oral and the nasal passage. There are no such nasalized vowels in English. Out of the 24 English consonants, 21 consonants are articulate through the oral passage. They are called *'oral'* consonants.

If the air is blocked in the oral passage and allowed to pass through the nasal passage by keeping the soft palate lowered, *'nasal'* consonants are produced. There are only *3 nasal* consonants, viz. /m/, /n/ and /   /.

(ii)   **Manipulation of Articulation :-** Manipulating the different articulatory organs is the second process to achieve the desired stricture. Articulatory organs are divided into two groups of

(a) Active Articulators and
(b) Passive Articulators.

Active articulators make a movement during the production of speech sounds and **passive articulators** are those articulatory organs towards which the

active articulators move. The lower lip
land the tongue arte active articulators.
The upper lip and the entire roof of the
mouth are passive articulators.

Having understood that we can now
discuss the consonants on the basis of the
manner of articulation :-

(a) Stop (or **Plosive**) **Consonants**
[complete closure & sudden release] :-
The active articulator makes a firm
contact with the passive articulator, and
thus prevents the lung-air to escape
through the mouth (**oral stop**).
Simultaneously (=At the same time) there
is a velic closure (**nasal stop**) so that the
nasal passage is blocked. Thus, the lung-
air gets compressed in the mouth. When
the active articulator is suddenly removed
from the passive articulator, the air comes
out through the oral passage with a small
explosion (burst). Therefore, *sounds
articulated with a stricture of complete
closure and sudden release are called*
plosives. There are six such plosives in
English. The initial sounds in the words
pin /p/, *bin* /b/ (bilabial), *tin* /t/, *din* /d/

(alveolar), *kin* /k/, and *gun* / / (velar) are
plosives.

There are two types of stop :-

(i) oral stop and
(ii)   nasal stop.

Therefore, when we talk about STOP
consonants, we mean a complete stoppage
of the airflow through both the nose and
the mouth. For only oral stop without the
nasal stop, the phoneticians use the term
NASAL consonants. If the term *stop*
appears confusing, the alternative *plosive*
can be conveniently used without any
confusion.

(b) Fricative Consonants [close
approximation] :- The active articulator
is brought so close to the passive
articulator that there is a very narrow gap
between them. The soft palate is raised so
as to shut off the nasal passage. The
lung-air is allowed to pass through the
narrow space between the two articulators
with slight **audible friction**. Such *sounds*
as are articulated with a stricture of close
approximation are termed **fricatives**.
The initial sounds in the English words

fine, vine, thin, then, sip, zip, sheep and *hat* as well as the final sound in *rouge* are fricatives. Thus, /f/, /v/ (labio-dental), /θ/, /ð/ (dental), /s/, /z/ (alveolar), /ʃ/, /ʒ/ (palato-alveolar), and /h/ (glottal)l are the nine fricatives in the R. P. Among these the two hissing sounds /s/ and /z/ are termed **sibilants**.

(c) Affricate [complete closure and slow release] **:-** These two sounds contain the qualities of both plosives and fricatives. The tip and blade of the tongue comes up to make contact with the back part of the alveolar ridge towards the hard palate to form an oral closure. The raised soft palate causes the velic nasal closure. The active articulator is removed slowly (*not suddenly*) from the passive articulator. Then, instead of the explosive noise (not like a plosive consonant), friction will be heard. This kind of combination of a plosive (complete closure) immediately followed by a fricative (slow release) is labelled as **affricate**. The initial consonants in *cheap* /tʃ/ and *just* /dʒ/ (palato-alveolar) are **affricates**. Also, notice that in the case of these two consonants only there are two symbols each for a single sound. The first symbol represents a plosive and the second represents a fricative. These symbols also help us to understand that there is a combination of a plosive and a fricative in an affricate.

(d) Lateral [partial closure] :- The tongue-tip and the sides of the tongue-blade are in firm contact with the alveolar ridge. But the sides of the remainder of the tongue are not in contact with the sides of the palate. Thus, this stricture obstructs the airstream in the centre of the oral passage but allows it to pass through the gap between the sides of the tongue and the palate. The velic closure does not allow the air to pass through the nasal passage. *Sounds that are articulated with a stricture of complete closure in the centre of the vocal tract but with the air escaping along the sides of the tongue without any friction are called* **laterals**. The initial sound in the English word *love* /l/ (alveolar) is a lateral. This is the only lateral consonant in English.

(e) Gliding Consonants (or Approximants) [open approximation] :- There are three consonants which consist of a quick, smooth, non-friction glide towards a following vowel sound. For their articulation the soft palate is raised to shut off the nasal passage. The active articulator is brought close to the passive articulator so that the gap between them is wide (not *narrow* as in **fricatives**). The air escapes through this gap without friction. *Sounds that are articulated with a stricture of open approximation are called* **semi-vowels** [/j/ and /w/] and **frictionless continuants**. It was Peter Ladefoged (1975) who used the term **approximants** for the sounds that are articulated with a stricture of open approximation.

The initial sound in *yes* /j/ is a quick glide from the position of the vowel /i:/ or / / (palatal) to the next vowel. Similarly, the initial sound in *weep* /w/ is a quick glide from the position of the vowel /u:/ or / / (bilabial) to the next vowel. Because both the consonants begin from the position of a vowel (but they are consonants), they are called **semi-vowels**.

The initial sound /r/ in the word *read* is the third gliding consonant, but it does not resemble any English vowel like /j/ or /w/. The tongue has a curved shape with the tip pointing towards the hard palate at the back of the alveolar ridge (**palato-alveolar**). The tongue-tip is not close enough to the palate to cause any friction. The soft palate is raised to close the nasal passage and the lung-air flows quietly between the tongue-tip and the palate without any friction. Therefore, this consonant is called **frictionless continuant**.

The letter **'r'** in English words like *red* and *ran* is pronounced as a **trill** by most Scottish people. **Trills** or **rolled consonants** are *sounds that are articulated with a stricture of intermittent closure*. To produce such a sound the soft palate is raised so that the nasal passage is shut off. Then the active articulator strikes against the passive articulator again and again. Thus, the air escapes between the two articulators intermittently. This is another variety of /r/ but not R.P.

There is yet another variety of the letter 'r' in the word *very*, which is pronounced as a **tap** or a **flap** by some English people. Again, this is not R.P. These varieties are well understood by the educated British speakers, but of course they sound foreign. In **taps** or **flaps** the active articulator strikes against the passive articulator just once (not several times as in **trills** or **rolled consonants**) and then quickly flaps forward.

Also, note that because there is no stoppage of air or friction in /l/, it is also included in the group of approximants and understood as **alveolar lateral approximant**. But it is usually called just **alveolar lateral** and its approximant status is just assumed.

(f) Nasal [complete oral closure] :- There are three nasal sounds in English. They are the terminal sounds in *ram, ran* and *rang*. In their articulation, the stricture is like that of the plosives, i.e. the active and passive articulators are in firm contact with each other. Thus, they block off the oral passage of air completely. But, unlike the plosives, the soft palate is not raised (i.e. kept lowered) so that the nasal passage of air remains open. *Sounds that are articulated with a stricture of complete oral closure are called* **nasals**. Notice that the places of articulation of these nasals [/m/ (bilabial), /n/ (alveolar), /   / (velar)] are the same as that of the three pairs of plosives.

(C) STATE OF GLOTTIS (or **POSITION OF VOCAL CORDS**) :- This is the third reference point to classify the consonants (or *to understand the difference between one consonant and another*). **Vocal cords** are a pair of lip-like structures in the larynx. They are positioned horizontally from front to back. They are attached at the front but can be separated at the back. The opening between the vocal cords is called the **glottis**. The **larynx** is also known as the **Adam's apple**. It is situated at the top of the windpipe. The air from the lungs has to pass through the windpipe and the larynx during **exhaling** (or *expiration*).

The vocal cords can be opened and closed because they can be separated at the back. When these vocal cords come very close to each other, the glottis is shut completely. When we swallow food or water, the vocal cords shut the glottis so that food or water may not enter the windpipe.

Normally the vocal cords are drawn apart and the glottis is open so that we can breathe in and out without any difficulty. The air enters the lungs and comes out through the wide open glottis. Some consonant sounds are also produced in this **position of the vocal cords** (or the *state of the glottis*). Such sounds produced with a wide open glottis are called **voiceless** (or **breathed sounds** *because this is the position of the vocal cords while breathing*). The initial sound in *pin, tin, kin, fin, thin, sin, shin, hat,* and *chin* are the nine **voiceless consonants** in English. Remember that the first consonant of each of the pairs of **plosives** [bilabial /p/, alveolar /t/ & velar /k/], **fricatives** [labio-dental /f/, dental / /, alveolar /s/, palato-alveolar / /, & glottal

/h/] and affricates [palato-alveolar /t /]
are **voiceless**. Voiceless glottal /h/ is a
single consoant sound (i.e. without a pair)
and has no **voiced** counterpart (or
partner).

On the other hand, during the
production of the remaining 15
consonants, the vocal cords are *loosely
held together* (i.e. brought close to each
other) and the pressure of the air from the
lungs makes them open and close rapidly.
This is called the vibration of the vocal
cords. So the sounds articulated when the
vocal cords vibrate are called **voiced**. All
the consonant sounds in the words *bad,
deal, girl, vine, then, zoo, measure, need,
wing, red, yarn*, and *jug* are <u>voiced</u>. That
is, /b/, /d/, / /, /v/, / /, /z/, / /, /d /, /l/,
/j/, /w/, /r/, /m/, /n/, and / / are the fifteen
voiced consonants. Keep in mind that all
vowel sounds are voiced. At the time of
whispering, all vowels and consonants
become voiceless.

The vibration of the vocal cords is
important for another factor also. The
speed at which the vocal cords vibrate is
called the **frequency** (of vibration of the

vocal cords) and this determines the **pitch** of the voice, which you will study about later.

It is possible to feel the difference between a voiceless and voiced sound. We can use one of the two ways for that. One, we can place our fingers lightly on the Adam's apple during the production of a certain sound. If the sound produced is voiced, our fingers will feel the vibration of the vocal cords. If the sound produced is voiceless, our fingers will feel nothing. For an example, if you produce a long *sssssssss* (i.e. a prolonged hissing sound) with your fingers on the Adam's apple, you do not feel any vibration. But, on the other hand, if you produce a long *zzzzzz* (i.e. a prolonged buzzing sound), your fingers will feel the vibration. That proves that the sibilant /s/ is **voiceless** but the buzzing /z/ is **voiced**.

Some people think the second method easier. The same two sounds can be produced again with your palms placed gently on your ears. A buzz is heard when *zzzzzzz* is produced but no such buzz is heard in the case of *sssssssss*.

These two ways can be repeated with
other sounds like *ffffffff* and *vvvvvvvv*.

On the basis of the three terms
discussed above we can very conveniently
label and remember that :-

/p/ is a **bilabial plosive voiceless**

and

/b/ is a **voiced bilabial plosive**.

Notice that there is no fixed rigid order
for the three terms used. Anyone of them
can precede or follow the other. These
three terms can be used very conveniently
to describe any consonant. Three terms
are also used to label the vowel sounds of
R.P. but they are different from the ones
used here.

PHONETICS - IV

--

Vowels : Unlike consonants, vowels are articulated with a stricture of pen approximation That is, during the production of vowels there is **no obstruction** in the oral passage (as there is during *plosives*, *affricates*, *lateral*, and *nasals*) or **no friction** (as there is during *fricatives*). There is sufficient gap between the active and passive articulators to allow the along-air to escape freely and continuously, **without any friction**.

The active articulator during the production of all vowels is (1) the front or (2) the centre or (3) the back of the tongue. The passive articulator is (a) the hard palate or (B) between back of hard palate and front of soft palate or (C) soft palate respectively. During the production of a vowel, the upper surface of the tongue is **convex** because some part of the tongue (front, central or back) is raised in the direction of the roof of the mouth.

There are 20 vowel sounds in English (R.P.). Out of them 12 are called *pure vowels* (or **monophthongs**) and 8 are called vowel glides (or **diphthongs**). Thus, on the basis of the part of the tongue that is highest in the mouth during the articulation of vowels, we can classify the pure vowels (=monophthongs) of English into three categories :-

(i) **Front vowels** (=during the articulation of which the front of the tongue is raised in the direction of the hard palate). The vowels in the English words *bee* /i:/, *bid* / /, *bed* /e/, and *bad* / / are the *four* front vowels.

(ii) **Back vowels** (=during the articulation o which the back of the tongue is raised in the direction of the soft palate). The vowels I the English words *cart* / :/, *cot* / /, *caught* / :/, *push* / /, and *pool* /u:/ are the **five** back vowels.

(iii) **Central vowels** (= during the articulation of which the centre of the tongue is raised in the direction of that part of the roof of the mouth where the hard palate and the soft palate meet). The underlined vowels in the English words *above* or   *teacher* / /, *heard* / :/ and *cup* / / are the **three** central vowels.

However, all the four front vowels /i:/, / /, /e/, and / / cannot be articulated in the same way. These vowels are produced by raising the front of tongue to different heights (or levels) with reference to the roof of the mouth. For producing /i:/ the tongue-front is the **nearest** to the hard palate and for / / it is the **farthest** from the hard palate. Thus, on the basis of the height to which the tongue-part is raised, we can have four levels (or heights) of the part(s) of the tongue raised, viz.

(a) **Close** (or **High**) vowels (=during the articulation of which a specific part of the tongue is closest (=nearest) to the roof of the mouth. The vowels in the English words *beach* /i:/ and *boot* /u:/ are examples of close vowels.

(b) **Open** (or **Low**) vowels (=during the articulation of which a specific part of the tongue is raised to a height farthest from the roof of the mouth). The vowels in the English words *part* / :/ and *pot* / / are open vowels.

(c) **Half-close** (or **Mid-high**) vowels are produced from a height between close and

open positions, but nearer to **close** that to
open position. The vowels in the English
words *sit* / / and *book* / / are examples
of half-close vowels.

(d) **Half-open** (or **Mid-low**) vowels are
produced from a height between close and
open positions, but nearer to **open** than to
close. The non-final vowel in the English
word s̲u̲bmit / / is a half-open vowel.

Keeping

(1) the part of the tongue raised and

(2) the height to which it is raised for the
articulation of vowels

we can have the following vowel-diagram
(=chart). Remember that this
quadrilateral refers to **cardinal vowels**.
These cardinal vowels do not actually
exist in any particular language of the
world. These are only reference points
which are used to study the vowels of
various languages and not of English
only. The area surrounded by the large
quadrilateral is called the **vowel-area**, i.e.
the area for the articulation of different
vowel sounds of different languages.

The 12 pure vowels of English have been marked in this vowel-diagram.

The vowel-diagram gives us two criteria for the classification of vowels. Yet there is one more criterion, i.e. the position of lips. According to this, the vowels are divided into two categories:-

(A) **Rounded vowels** (=during the articulation of which the lips are rounded. The vowels in the English words *shop* / /, *horse* / :/, *pull* / /, and *cool* /u:/ are the four rounded vowels.

(B) **Unrounded vowels** (=during the production of which the lips are spread or neutral, but not rounded). The remaining eight monophthongs are unrounded.

To summarise, a vowel is studied through the following three criteria:-

(I) The part of the tongue raised during its articulation (fsront, central, back)

(II)   The height to which it is raised (close, half-close, half-open, open)

(III)   The position of the lips (rounded, unrounded)

Now, we can take up the 12 pure vowels (monophthongs) one by one with its three-term labels and its occurrence in English words. Pay special attention to the spellings because different letters (or their combinations) give different sounds. This is the problem of the English language, which has to manage 44 sounds with 26 letters of the alphabet.

/iː/   **front close unrounded**

initially → eat, eel, eke

medially →beat, feel, geyser, seize, receive

terminally → bee, key, she, pea

/ /   **front half-close unrounded**

initially → it, if, in

medially → lid, rich, busy

terminally → city, recipe, semi

/e/**front unrounded between half-close and half-open**

initially → any, enemy, egg

medially →bed, pest, then

terminally → It does not occur finally
in English words.

**/ /   front unrounded just below
half-open**

initially → axe, apple, ass

medially →bat, chap, hat

terminally → It does not occur
terminally in English words.

/ :/   back open unrounded vowel

initially → <u>ar</u>t, <u>au</u>nt, <u>a</u>fter

medially →p<u>a</u>st, f<u>ar</u>m, cl<u>a</u>ss

finally → c<u>ar</u>, b<u>aa</u>, sp<u>a</u>

/ /   back rounded (just above the)
open (position)

initially → <u>ho</u>nour, <u>o</u>ff, <u>o</u>ften

medially → shot, pod, gone

terminally → It does not occur finally.

**/ :/   back rounded vowel between
half-open and half-close**

initially ➔ <u>ou</u>ght, <u>a</u>ll, <u>Au</u>gust

medially ➔ h<u>oa</u>rd, f<u>a</u>ll, f<u>ou</u>ght, f<u>au</u>lt

finally ➔ l<u>aw</u>, m<u>ore</u>, f<u>our</u>

/ /   **back rounded** (just above) **half-close**

initially ➔ It does not occur in the beginning of English words, except *"oomph"*.

medially ➔ put, sugar, book

terminally ➔ Only in unaccented (weak) preposition *"to"*

/u:/   **back close rounded** vowel

initially ➔ ooze, oodles

medially ➔ pool, shoed, boots

terminally ➔ zoo, shoe, to

/ :/   **central unrounded** vowel
between half-close & half-open

initially ➔ <u>ir</u>k, <u>ear</u>ly, <u>ur</u>n

medially ➔ b<u>ur</u>n, f<u>ir</u>st, h<u>ear</u>d

terminally ➔ mons<u>ieur</u>, meiss<u>ieurs</u>

/ /   (when final) **central unrounded**
(just below) **half-open**

finally → teach<u>er</u>, sof<u>a</u>, hon<u>our</u>

/ /   (when non-final) **central
unrounded between half-close & half-
open**

*[It is exactly like / :/. The only
difference is that it is short.]*

initially → <u>a</u>bove, <u>u</u>tmost, <u>a</u>part

medially → s<u>u</u>bmit, p<u>er</u>mit, c<u>o</u>mpare

/ /   **central unrounded** vowel
between half-open & open

initially → <u>u</u>nder, <u>u</u>p, <u>u</u>ncle

medially → c<u>u</u>p, d<u>o</u>ne, h<u>u</u>nt

terminally → It does not occur.

Out of these 12 pure vowels, 5 are long
while remaining 7 are short. The colon
sign (:) after the symbols indicates length.
Thus, the five vowels /i:/, / :/, / :/, /u:/,
and / :/ are long.

Besides this length in general, every vowel (monophthong or diphthong) is relatively longer when it is <u>word-ending</u> or <u>followed by a voiced consonant</u> than <u>when it is followed by a voiceless consonant</u>. For example, /i:/ is longer in *'bee'* or *'beam'* than in *'beat'* and / / is longer in *'bow'* or *'bowl'* than in *'bout'*. In a diphthong, it is the first element that is made long while the second element is very short.

Like monophthongs, 8 diphthongs have been shown in the following diagram.

The dot shows the beginning and the arrow indicates the direction of the vowel glide. Notice that a diphthong is a combination of two vowel sounds (as the symbols suggest) but is considered to be a single sound (phoneme). Diphthongs can be put into 3 groups :-

(i) ending in / /

(ii)   ending in / /

(iii)   ending in / /. Let us take them up one by one.

/e /   from **front unrounded just below half-close** to **front unrounded** vowel **just above half-close**

initially → eight, aim, age

medially → gate, straight, freight

terminally → pay, they, café

/ /   from **front open unrounded** to **centralized front unrounded vowel just above half-close**

initially → ice, aisle, eyes

medially → price, type, sight, tied

terminally → pie, dye, cry

/ /   from **back rounded vowel between open & half-open** to **front unrounded vowel just above half-close**

initially → oil, syster

medially → choice, coin, foyer

terminally → boy, joy, annoy

/   /   from **central unrounded vowel between half-close & half-open** to **centralized back rounded vowel just above half-close**

initially → open, only, own, aubergine

medially → moan, quote, host, chauffeur

terminally → go, foe, low, though

/   /   from **back open unrounded** to **back half-close rounded**

initially → owl, out, ouch

medially → fowl, bout, sound

terminally → how, cow, slough

/   /   from centralized front unrounded just above half-close to

(1) **central unrounded between half-close & half-open**, if non-final
(2) **central unrounded just below half-open**, if final

initially → ears, eerie

medially ➔ merely, filial, union, beard, fierce

terminally ➔ here, sheer, fear, ar<u>ea</u>

/ /   from **front half-open unrounded** to

(1) central unrounded between half-close & half-open, if non-final

(2) central unrounded just below half-open, if final

initially ➔ airy, area, aerodrome

medially ➔ wary, shared, fairy, bears

terminally ➔ hair, declare, there, tear

/ /   from **centralized back rounded just above half-close** to

(1) central unrounded between half-close & half-open, if non-final

(2) central unrounded just below half-open, if final

initially ➔ It does not occur.

medially ➔ purely, Europe, gourd

terminally → poor, sure, you're, bluer

PHONETICS - V

--

We had a mere reference to the organs of speech divided into three groups of respiratory, phonatory and articulatory systems. We can now study them in a slightly detailed manner but we shall go in the order of the above-mentioned three groups.

1. **Respiratory system** involves the lungs, the chest muscles, the windpipe, the pharynx, and the nose. The **lungs** are a

pair of spongy bag-like bodies. They are made of small sacs called the **alveoli** (singular *'alveolus'*). In these sacs, blood is cleaned of its carbon-dioxide and provided with fresh oxygen from the outer air. Air is supplied to the alveoli by small tubes called the **bronchioles**. The bronchioles come together into two large tubes called the **bronchi** (singular *'bronchus'*), one on the right and the other on the left. These bronchi join the **windpipe** (or *'trachea'*). It is through the windpipe that the air we breathe in passes through the throat into the lungs. The act of respiration (breathing) involves two processes—taking outer air into (*breathing in*) the lungs [called *'inspiration'* or *'inhaling'*] and throwing out air (breathing out) from the lungs into the atmosphere [called *'expiration'* or *'exhaling'*]. It is the expiratory lung-air that is used for the articulation of most speech sounds of all languages. This air-stream involving lung-air is called **pulmonic air-stream**.

An air-stream is produced by an air-stream mechanism. This air-stream mechanism works exactly in the same way as a flit-gun does. In a flit-gun, a body of liquid (or air if it is empty) is moved by working an apparatus (which is a part of the flit-gun) called a plunger. When the plunger is moved in one direction, the liquid (or air) is pulled in and when it is moved in the opposite direction, the liquid (or air) is pushed out. When we speak, something like the plunger in a flit-gun, works in the same way. This is called the **initiator**. The air-stream is set in motion by the initiator, just as the liquid in a flit-gun is set in motion by the plunger.

The pulmonic air-stream mechanism consists of the lungs and the respiratory muscles (chest muscles). The walls of the lungs act as the initiator. They are moved by the respiratory muscles so that the air is drawn into the lungs or pushed out of them. When this air-stream mechanism is used to push air out, it is called *egressive* and when it is used to draw air in, it is termed *ingressive*.

As mentioned earlier, most speech sounds make use of **pulmonic egressive** air-stream mechanism. In fact, all the sounds of English are produced with this air-stream mechanism. It is possible to articulate speech sounds using pulmonic ingressive air-stream mechanism, but no language uses it. It is used for yawning and snoring, but not for speaking.

PHONETICS – VI

1. What was the purpose of the Arab grammarians in studying   sounds of Arabic?

2. How did they do that?

3. What does phonetics study?

4. What is the speech chain?

5. What are the three branches of phonetics?

6. What is acoustic phonetics?

7. What is auditory phonetics?

8. What is articulatory phonetics?

9. What are the three divisions of the organs of speech?

10. How are the organs of speech divided into?

11. What does the respiratory system include?

12. What does the phonatory system comprise?

13. What does the articulatory system consist of?

14. How is the ear very important for the speech production?

15. How many speech sounds (phonemes) are there in the R.P.?

16. How many vowels are there in the R.P.?

17. How many consonants are there in the R.P.?

18. How many oral sounds/consonants/vowels are there in the R.P.?

19. How many nasal sounds/consonants/vowels are there in the R.P.?

20. How many voiced sounds/consonants/vowels are there in the R.P.?

21. How many voiceless sounds/consonants/vowels?

22. How is a vowel sound produced?

23. How is a consonant produced?

24. How can we describe how a speech sound is produced?

25. What are the three criteria that the consonants are studied through?

26. What is meant by:

-The place of articulation?

-The manner of articulation?

-The position of the vocal cords?

27. What are the three positions that a vowel can have in a word?

28. Some speech sounds can't occur in all
positions. Give examples.

29. How many places of articulation are
there for the production of the
consonants?

30. How is the sound produced if it is:

-Bilabial?

-Labio-dental?

-Dental?

-Alveolar?

-Palato-alveolar?

-Palatal?

-Velar?

-Glottal?

31. What are the places of articulation for
the vowel sounds?

32. How many bilabial sounds are there?

33. How many labio-dental sounds are
there?

34. How many dental sounds are there?

35. How many alveolar sounds are there?

36. How many palato-alveolar sounds are there?

37. How many palatal sounds are there?

38. How many velar sounds are there?

39. How many glottal sounds are there?

40. When do we call the sound /r/ as linking /r/?

41. What is the other name of?

-Palato-alveolar consonant.

-The larynx.

-The R.P.

-The vocal folds.

-Stop consonants.

-Gliding consonant.

-Exhaling.

42. What does the term "stricture" mean?

43. How is this stricture achieved?

44. How can speech sounds be classified as "oral" or "nasal"?

45. What is meant by the velic closure?

46. What kind of sound is produced if the air is blocked in the oral passage and allowed to pass through the nasal passage only? (Or) When are the nasal sounds produced?

47. What are the nasal sounds in English?

48. What are the oral sounds in English?

49. Articulatory organs are divided into two groups. What are they?

50. What is meant by active and passive articulators?

51. What are the active articulators?

52. What are the passive articulators?

53. What kind of closure is involved in the production of:

-Stop (or plosive) consonant?

-Fricative consonants?

-Affricates?

-Laterals?

-Gliding?

-Nasal consonants?

54. Write which manner of articulation it is from the type of stricture:

-A stricture of complete closure and sudden release.

-A stricture of close approximation.

-A stricture of complete closure and slow release.

-A stricture of partial closure.

-A stricture of open approximation.

-A stricture of complete oral closure.

55. When it is an oral stop?

56. When it is a nasal stop?

57. For what kind of stops do the phoneticians use the term nasal consonants?

58. What are the two types of stop?

59. What is the alternative name for the term "stop"?

60. Why is the soft palate raised for the production of the fricatives?

61. The fricatives are produced with a stricture of close approximation; how can that be achieved?

62. What causes the velic closure?

63. Say which place of articulation it is?

-From/with two lips.

-Lip and teeth.

-From/with teeth.

-From/with the teeth ridge.

-From with hard palate and alveolar ridge.

-From/with the hard palate.

-From/with the velum or soft palate.

-From/with glottis.

64. Say which manner of articulation it is?

-Complete closure and sudden release.

-Close approximation.

-Complete closure and slow release.

-Partial closure.

-Open approximation.

-Complete oral closure.

65. What are the vocal cords?

66. What is the glottis?

67. What do we call the sounds that are
produced with a wide open glottis?

PHONETICS - VII

--

Earlier we studied that half of our body
is involved during speech and that many
organs are used to produce different
sounds. But we had a mere reference to

these *organs of speech* divided into three groups of respiratory, phonatory and articulatory systems. We can now study them in a slightly detailed manner but we shall go in the order of the above-mentioned three groups. But before that look at Figure 1, which shows different parts used in the articulation of speech sounds.

1. Respiratory system is mainly used for breathing but it is also used for speaking. For speech production we need an air-stream. The air going out of the lungs provides energy for producing various speech sounds. This system involves the lungs, the chest muscles, the windpipe, the pharynx, and the nose. Here two things need to be noted. First, that an organ belonging to one system, e.g. the nose, can be repeated in another system, e.g. the articulatory system, also. Secondly, some organs help directly, and some indirectly, in the production of speech.

The **lungs** are a pair of spongy balloon-like bodies. They are made of small sacs called the **alveoli** (singular *'alveolus'*). In these sacs, blood is cleaned of its carbon-dioxide and provided with fresh oxygen from the outer air. Air is supplied to the alveoli by small tubes called the **bronchioles**. The bronchioles come together into two large tubes called the **bronchi** (singular *'bronchus'*), one on the right and the other on the left. Each bronchus joins the **windpipe** (or *'trachea'*) to the lungs. It is through the windpipe that the air we breathe in passes through the throat into the lungs. The windpipe is in front of the foodpipe (oesophagus). The act of respiration (breathing) involves two processes— taking outer air into (*breathing in*) the lungs [called *'inspiration'* or *'inhalation'*] and throwing out air *(breathing out)* from the lungs into the atmosphere [called *'expiration'* or *'exhalation'*]. It is the expiratory lung-air that is used for the articulation of most speech sounds of all languages. It provides the energy needed for the articulation of speech sounds. You must have realised that when this energy is exhausted while speaking, we have to stop in order to breathe in and out

to speak again. This air-stream involving lung-air is called **pulmonic air-stream**.

The pulmonic air-stream mechanism consists of the lungs and the respiratory muscles (chest muscles). The walls of the lungs are moved by the respiratory muscles so that the air is drawn into the lungs or pushed out of them. When this air-stream mechanism is used to push air out, it is called *egressive*; and when it is used to draw air in, it is termed *ingressive*.

As mentioned earlier, most speech sounds make use of **pulmonic egressive** air-stream mechanism. In fact, all the sounds of English are produced with this air-stream mechanism. It is possible to articulate speech sounds using **pulmonic ingressive** air-stream mechanism, but no language uses it. It is used for yawning and snoring, but not for speaking.

2. Phonatory system is responsible for supplying the musical note or *'voice'* to the speech sound. On the basis of the presence of 'voice', some sounds are called 'voiced'. Those sounds are called 'voiceless' whose articulation is without 'voice'. This system comprises the larynx and the vocal folds (or **cords**) inside it. You have already read that during whispering, all sounds become voiceless. Therefore, it is not possible to sing in the whispering mode because no musical notes can be added to the singer's voice.

Larynx is the upper part of the windpipe where the vocal cords are found. It is perceived as the most important part of the mechanism of speech production, because it is the generator (source) of speech sounds, particularly the voiced sounds produced by the vibration of the vocal cords. The air released from the lungs comes up through the windpipe and arrives first at the larynx, which is the independent producer of <u>voice</u>, i.e. voiced sounds. The larynx contains two small bands of elastic tissues, which can be thought of as two flat strips of rubber lying opposite each other across the air passage. These are the **vocal cords**. They are positioned horizontally from front to back. The vocal cords are attached at the front but can be separated at the back. The inner edges of the vocal cords can be moved towards each other so that they meet and completely cover the top of the windpipe; or they can be held apart so that there is a gap between them, known as the *glottis*, through which the air can pass freely. This is the usual position of the vocal cords when we breathe quietly in and out. Figure 2 clearly indicates the various parts of the phonatory system.

When the vocal cords are brought together tightly, no air can pass through them and if the lungs are pushing air from below, this air gets compressed. If the vocal cords are then opened suddenly, the compressed air bursts out with a sort of coughing noise. Such holding back of the compressed air followed by a sudden release is called the glottal stop; and what we feel as the air bursts out is the vocal cords springing apart.

However, if the vocal cords are brought together quite gently, the air from the lungs will be able to force them apart for a moment, but then they will return to the closed position again; then the air will force them apart again, and they will close again, and so on. This is a very rapid process and may take place as many as 800 to 1500 times per second in male-voice and from 1200 to 1900 times per second in female-voice. Obviously, it is not possible to hear each individual 'click' of the opening and closing of vocal cords. What we actually hear is a musical note. The note, whether high or low, produced by this rapid opening and closing of vocal cords is called '**voice**'. Some of the English sounds have voice are called '*voiced*'. All the vowel sounds are voiced and 15 consonants are also voiced. The sounds which are not voiced are called '*voiceless*'; and are produced with the vocal cords drawn apart so that the air can pass out freely between them without vibration. 9 consonants are voiceless. The difference between voiced and voiceless is important to distinguish between what are otherwise similar sounds, e.g. voiced /z/ and voiceless /s/. All this and a few other things related with the phonatory system have already been discussed under the heading "STATE OF GLOTTIS or POSITION OF

VOCAL CORDS". Read that again for better understanding of the system.

3. Articulatory system is the system which is chiefly related with the articulation of speech sounds. The organs of speech above the larynx are called **articulators**. On that score, we can term the organs of respiratory system as '**respirators**' and those of phonatory system as '**phonators**'.

The passage of air above the larynx is known as the '**vocal tract**'. From the uvula this vocal tract gets divided into (a) '**oral tract**' below the uvula extending to the lips; and (b) '**nasal tract**' above the uvula extending to the nose. Raising or lowering the velum (called '*oro-nasal process*') controls the oral and nasal tracts to produce oral and nasal sounds.

We have already discussed the difference between the *active* articulators and *passive* articulators. You will realise that the *lower* articulators are active and *upper* articulators are passive. The articulators can also be divided into further two groups of *movable* and *unmovable.* Now we can discuss these articulators one by one.

(a) **Pharynx** is the cavity at the top of the throat which connects nasal and oral passages on one side and oesophagus (foodpipe) and larynx on the other side. In other words, it is the hollow area just above the larynx up to the entrance of the oral or nasal cavities. It is about 8 centimetres in men and 7 centimetres in women. At the top end it is divided into two parts : one being the back of the mouth and the other beginning of the way to the nasal cavity.

(b) **Soft Palate** (or **Velum**) is a muscular flap that can be raised to press against the back wall of the pharynx and shut off the nasal tract, thus preventing air from going out through the nose. This action is called *velic closure.* It separates the nasal tract from the oral tract so that the air can pass only through the mouth. At the lower end of the velum is a small appendage hanging down, called the uvula. The part of the vocal tract between the uvula and the larynx is the pharynx. Thus, the back wall of the pharynx may be considered to be one of the articulators on the upper surface of the vocal tract. The velum is an articulator in two ways : (i) when it is raised, the airstream coming from the lungs through the larynx cannot escape through the nose; (ii) it can be touched by the tongue to produce certain sounds. To produce the sounds /k/, / / and / / the back of the tongue is in contact with the lower side of the velum. Therefore, we call these sounds <u>velar sounds</u> or <u>velar consonants</u>.

(c) **Hard Palate** (or **Palate**) : The palate forms the roof of the mouth and separates the mouth/oral cavity from the nose/nasal cavity. When we make the tip of the tongue touch as much of our palate as we can, we feel that most of it is hard and fixed. But when the tongue-tip goes as far back as it can go, away from the teeth, we notice that the palate becomes soft. The hard fixed part of the palate is divided into two sections : the <u>alveolar/teeth ridge</u> and the <u>hard palate</u>. The hard palate is the highest part of the palate between the alveolar ridge and the beginning of the velum. The hard palate, curving downwards towards the teeth at each side, is the front part of the mouth formed by a bony structure. During the articulation of the semi-vowel /j/, the front of the tongue comes close to the hard palate, allowing a gap to produce sound without any friction. Therefore, this sound is called palatal. Because the soft palate is called velum, the hard palate can simply be called the palate without any confusion.

(d) **Alveolar Ridge** (or **Teeth Ridge** or **Alveolum**) : Just behind the upper teeth there is a small protuberance that can be felt with the tip of the tongue. This is covered with little ridges. It is called the alveolar/teeth ridge and is specially important in English because many of the consonants like /t/, /d/, /n/, /l/, /r/, /s/, /z/, / /, / /, /t /, /d / are produced with the tongue touching or being close to the alveolar ridge.

(e) **Tongue** is the most important articulatory organ because it has the greatest variety of movements. Although it has no natural divisions like the palate, it is convenient to think of it as divided

into five parts. The <u>tip and blade</u> of the
tongue are the most mobile parts. The tip
and the blade lie under the alveolar
ridge—the tip being the most forward part
of all and the blade between the tip and
the front of the tongue. Behind the blade
lies what is technically called the <u>front</u> of
the tongue : it is actually the forward part
of the tongue and lies underneath the hard
palate when the tongue is at rest. The
remainder of the tongue can be divided
into the <u>centre</u> (which is partly beneath
the hard palate and partly beneath the
velum), the <u>back</u> (which is beneath the
soft palate when the tongue is at rest) and
the <u>root</u> (which is opposite the back wall
of the pharynx). The epiglottis is attached
to the lower part of the root of the tongue.
Because of this mobile and elastic nature
of the tongue, it is very important in
producing many consonants and vowels
as well.

(f) Teeth : The lower front teeth
are not important in speech production
except that if they are missing, certain
sounds (e.g. /s/ and /z/) will be difficult to
articulate. But the two upper front teeth

are used in English. When we put the tip of the tongue very close to the edge of these teeth and blow, it will produce a sound like / / as in the English word *thin*. If we turn on the voice *(by bringing the vocal cords closer to produce voiced sounds)* during this / / sound, we shall get a sound like / / as in the English word *then*. Such sounds, made with the tongue touching the front upper teeth are called <u>dental</u>.

(g) Lips are obviously important in speech since they can take up various shapes : (1) they can be pressed together firmly to block the air passage through the mouth to produce sounds like /p/, /b/ and /m/; (2) the lower lip can be drawn inward and moved slightly upward to bring in contact with the upper front teeth to articulate the sounds /f/ and /v/; (3) they can be rounded with different amounts as in /uː/, / / or /w/; (4) they can be kept apart in flat unrounded positions as in /e/ or / /; (5) they can be spread as in /iː/; or (6) they can be pushed forward to a greater or lesser extent for certain sounds. Sounds like /p/, /b/, /m/, or /w/, in which both lips are in contact with each other or rounded, are technically called <u>bilabial</u>.

The seven articulators described above are the major articulators used in the production of speech sounds, yet there are three marginal ones which can be considered articulators because they are essential for making certain types of sounds.

(h) **Jaws** are not directly involved in the articulation of sounds but they, too, are active and operative in order to give different shapes needed to produce various sounds.

(i) **Nose** has already been mentioned in the respiratory system because it is mainly used for breathing. However, the nasal cavity is very important while articulating *nasal* sounds, e.g. /m/, /n/ and / / in English. For producing a nasal consonant, the air is prevented from going out through the mouth, e.g. by closing the two lips for /m/. Because the soft palate is kept lowered, the air can pass through the nose to make a nasal sound. For oral sounds the velum is raised to block the nasal passage, known as the *velic closure*. Also, in some languages, like Hindi and French, the vowels are nasalized by allowing the air to go out through both the mouth and the nose.

(j) The importance of the **EAR** in checking, controlling and correcting our own speech was explained in the handout titled 'Phonetics–I'. We are not going to repeat it. Nevertheless, the main value of the ear in relation to the listener is the field of 'Auditory Phonetics', which you will study later.

Thus, we have learnt the significance of the various organs in producing the sounds of a language, which comes under 'Articulatory Phonetics'. The following brief descriptions of a few organs already mentioned will also be helpful.

Windpipe : It is the passage of air from lungs to the throat. Technically it is known as '*trachea*'.

Epiglottis : It is the small flat part at the root of the tongue, which is lowered

during swallowing to prevent food, etc.
from entering the windpipe.

Uvula : It is a small piece of fleshy matter
dangling/hanging from the back of the
velum.

Oesophagus : It is the tube at the bottom
of pharynx which takes food to the
stomach.

PHONETICS - VIII

--

Word stress in English is something
unpredictable and confusing. However,
there are a few important rules, which are
helpful, regarding word stress. They are
given below with examples:-

Rule 1 : Words with weak prefixes have
the stress on the ROOT and NOT on the
prefix, e.g.

a'bed; a'loud; a'far;

be'little; be'friend; em'bitter;

en'rich; dis'loyal; dis'honest;

Rule 2 : The inflectional suffixes *–ed* (to make past & past participle forms of verbs), *–er, -es* (to derive comparative & superlative degrees of adjectives/adverbs), *-s, -es* (to obtain singular present form of verbs), and *-ing* (to form present participial/gerundial form of verbs) do not affect the stress. That is, words to which these suffixes are added have the stress on the SAME SYLLABLE as before, e.g.

de'feated;   de'veloped; 'benefited;
sepa'rated; con'ducted; 'conquered;
'happier;

'unkindest;   'bandages; for'bids;
de'manding; 'auditing;

Rule 3 : The derivational suffixes *–age, –ance, –ant, –en, –er, –ess, –ful, –hood, –ish, –ive, –less, –ly, –ment, –ness, –or, –ship,* do NOT change the stress pattern. The root words and the new words formed by adding these suffixes have the stress on SAME syllable, e.g.

'coverage;   at'tendance; as'sistant;
brighten;   pro'ducer; 'waitress;
'dutiful;

'motherhood;   'yellowish;   a'busive;
'colourless; 'certainly;   a'chievement;

'loveliness;   col'lector;   'scholarship;
en'viable;   'capable;

Rule 4 : Words ending with *–ion, –ic, –ical, –ial, –ically, –ity, –icide, –logy, –ious, –tomy, –cracy, –graphy* have the primary stress on the syllable immediately preceding the suffix, e.g.

'nation; in'vasion;   in'flexion;
ecclesi'astic;   me'chanical; confi'dential;

psycho'logically;   elec'tricity;
in'secticide;   anthro'pology;
pre'carious;

appen'dectomy;   aris'tocracy;
pho'tography;

Rule 5 : Words ending with *–ate* take the stress two syllables before it, e.g.

'celebrate;   com'municate;
par'ticipate;

Rule 6 : Words ending with the suffixes –
ee, –self, –selves, –ever take the stress on
the suffixes themselves, e.g.

**devo'tee;   consig'nee; your'self;
our'selves;   whoso'ever;**

Rule 7 : In the case of conversion, when
the same word functions as a
noun/adjective and a verb, generally the
stress is in the beginning for the
noun/adjective, which shifts to the second
syllable for verbs, e.g.

**'produce (n);   pro'duce (v); 'present
(n/adj);   pre'sent (v);   'export (n);
ex'port (v);**

PHONETICS IX

There are 5 stages communication
are : psychological (idea & encoding),
articulatory (physiological articulation),
acoustic (physical transmission), auditory

(physiological audition), & cognition
(decoding & comprehension).

Half of our body (from head to
abdomen) is needed to produce sounds :
respiratory (trunk), phonatory (throat) and
articulatory (head).

Organs of Speech : Lips, Teeth,
Teeth/Alveolar Ridge (convex part of the
roof of the mouth behind the upper teeth),
Hard Palate (concave part of the roof of
the mouth behind the teeth ridge), Soft
Palate (flexible part at the back of the roof
of the mouth, which can be lowered or
raised), Uvula (end of the soft palate),
Pharynx (space between the back of the
tongue & back wall of the throat), Blade
of Tongue including Tip (part lying
opposite teeth ridge when tongue is at
rest), Front of Tongue (part lying opposite
hard palate when tongue is at rest), Back
of Tongue (part lying opposite soft palate
when tongue is at rest), Root of Tongue,
Epiglottis (small flat part at back of
tongue closing while swallowing to
prevent anything to go into the windpipe),
Windpipe, Larynx (situated at top of
windpipe with a pair of vocal cords, seen

in adult males as Adam's apple), Vocal Folds (pair of lip-like structure placed front to back horizontally in the larynx), & Glottis (space between vocal cords).

Sounds produced with the glottis open is said to be **voiceless** or **breathed**.

The opening and closing action of vocal cords is 100-150 per second in a man's voice & 200-325 in a woman's voice. This vibration of vocal cords produces **voiced** sounds & constitutes the process of **phonation**.

If you want to observe the part of the mouth (lips, teeth, alveolar ridge, hard palate, soft palate, uvula, tongue, & pharynx), look into a mirror with your mouth open.

In normal breathing the soft palate is kept lowered so that the air can escape through the nose & the mouth. This is the position of the velum in the *oro-nasal process* while producing **voiceless** & **nasalized** sounds. When the soft palate is raised, the nasal passage is closed, and we get the velic closure, which is necessary for **oral** sounds (unlike **nasal** sounds).

Nasal sounds are produced when the velum is lowered & the oral passage is shut off by an obstruction in the mouth.

The lips can have five positions : spread, neutral, open, close rounded, & open rounded. **Rounded** & **unrounded** lip-positions are important for description of vowels.

The tongue assumes different positions for the articulation of consonant & vowel sounds. For convenience we can refer to **tip**, **blade**, **front**, & **back** of the tongue.

In **re-entered**, *e* has 4 different pronunciations, including one silent letter. The letter-string **ough** is pronounced in 8 different ways in *bough, bought, cough, dough, hiccough, rough, thorough, & through*. George Bernard Shaw fabricated the peculiar word **ghoti** for *fish* : using **gh** as in *enough,* **o** as in *women,* & **ti** as in *nation.* As per one estimate, about 80% of English words are not spelled phonetically. As a solution to this kind of a problem, the symbols of the International Phonetic Alphabet (IPA), as

set out and explained in The Principles of
the International Phonetic Association,
are used to transcribe the sounds of any
language. This is a convenient device
because one symbol represents only one
sound. Transcriptions are of two kinds :
broad/phonemic and narrow/phonetic.
All the consonants are common in Daniel
Jones' *English Pronouncing Dictionary*
(EPD) 14th edition, A. S. Hornby's *The
Advanced Learner's Dictionary of
Current English* (ALD) 4th edition, and A.
C. Gimson's *An Introduction to the
Pronunciation of English* 4th revised
edition (1989). However, in the case of
the vowels, only one symbol **ɛə** as in *fair*

is used specially by A. C. Gimson as
against **eə** used by EPD or ALD. DO

NOT use the phonetic symbols as you
like. The mark ['] before a syllable means
that the syllable is stressed. DO learn
these symbols carefully. A good way of
learning them is to transcribe a few words
everyday & check the transcribed in a
dictionary.

PHONETICS : The Arab grammarians studied the sounds of Arabic in a very systematic (scientific) way. Their main purpose was to preserve the correct pronunciation of the Quran (Qoran, Koran) and to prevent it from any mispronunciation. They described the sounds and also gave detailed descriptions of the organs of speech. As early as in the beginning of the 4th century B.C. the grammarians of Greece and China studied the sounds of their respective languages. Before them an Indian grammarian named Panini also studied the sounds of Sanskrit (c. 5th century B.C.) at the University of Taxila (now in Pakistan). He is said to be the first phonetician. Their descriptions are very much like what we study today in general phonetics.

Phonetics studies the speech sounds (i.e. **human**, because animal sounds cannot be called so although their sounds may have certain meanings) of the languages of the world. Phonetics is divided into three branches on the basis of the three stages of speech production (articulation), transmission and reception,

which is known as the *speech chain*.
(**Articulatory** → **Acoustic** →
Auditory)

Articulatory Phonetics deals with the physiological stage of speech production. The speaker's speech organs move in a specific way for every sound. This stage of phonetics studies these movements. It shows how each sound is articulated (produced).

The domain of **Acoustic Phonetics** is the physical stage of speech transmission. The acoustic stage follows the articulatory stage. The sounds produced by the speaker disturb the air and cause sound waves like the waves of water in a lake or a sea. Every speech sound has a different sound wave from the other. This stage of phonetics studies these sound waves. It examines them and gives their characteristics.

Auditory Phonetics studies the physiological stage of speech reception. The hearer's auditory organs receive sound waves which travel through the sensory nerves to the brain and the brain understands the sound waves as the sounds of the language (linguistic form). This stage is difficult to understand because some parts of this system are still a mystery to science.

For our study articulatory phonetics is the most important. Therefore, we shall study how speech sounds are produced. In speech production more than half of our body is needed and used. Different organs of our body come into action while producing speech sounds. The lungs, the muscles of the chest, the larynx, the lips, the mouth, etc. are used to produce speech sounds. These organs are called the *organs of speech.*

The expression (term) "**organs of speech**" is not very suitable because all these organs are not used primarily for speech. They have functions other than the production of speech. The lungs are necessary for breathing, the teeth are used for chewing food, the tongue is needed for the difference in tastes, etc. But for want of a better expression, the phoneticians continue to call them the *organs of speech.*

These organs of speech are divided into
three groups according to their functions
:-

Respiratory System includes the lungs,
the chest muscles, the windpipe (or
trachea), the pharynx, and the nose.

Phonatory System comprises the larynx
and the vocal folds (or *cords*) inside it.
The vocal folds are the sound source.

Ariculatory System consists of the lips,
the teeth, the roof of the mouth, the
tongue, the pharynx, and the nose.

The ear, too, is very important for
speech production. The speaker is also
the listener to his own speech. He hears
and controls his own sounds while he
pronounces them. People who become
deaf due to some disease or accident
cannot hear their own speech. Therefore,
they slowly lose the ability to speak and
at last become dumb as well as deaf.
Thus, hearing ourselves is also important
as we speak. In phonetics, we call this the
"feedback link". It means that the
speaker's speech again enters his own

ears and helps him to check, control and
correct his mistakes.

Now, here is a total number of 44
speech sounds (phonemes) in the **R.P.**
(i.e. Received Pronunciation). R.P. is also
known as the **B.B.C. English** or **Queen's
English.** It is the variety of English
spoken by the educated British speakers.

Out of these 44 speech sounds, 20
are vowels and 24 are consonants. A
vowel sound is produced orally (not
nasally) without any stricture, i.e. closure
or partial closure. There is a free flow of
air-stream from the lungs.

A consonant sound is articulated
with some kind of stricture (closure) in
the path of the air-stream. It is easier to
explain how a consonant is produced.
Phoneticians give three-term labels to
both vowels and consonants. These labels
are very convenient to learn. On the basis
of these three-term labels we can easily
describe how a speech sound is produced.

A consonant is studied on the basis of the following three criteria (singular "criterion") :-

(1) Place of Articulation, i.e. from which place the consonant is articulated

(2) Manner of Articulation, i.e. the type of the stricture used to articulate a specific consonant

(3) Position of Vocal Cords (or **Folds),** i.e. whether they are held apart or brought closer.

We can take these reference points one by one and see how consonants differ from one another in relation to each one of them. Further, it is important to understand that the speech sounds can have three positions in a word :-

(iv)   initial, i.e. in the beginning

(v)   medial, i.e. in a position when it has some sound(s) before and also some sound(s) after it

(vi)   terminal, i.e. at the end.

Therefore, we shall try to find examples of words where the specific sound occurs

initially, medially and terminally. We
need to keep in mind that some speech
sounds may not occur in all the three
positions, e.g. no word in English ends
with /h/ or no word begins with / /.

(A) PLACE OF ARTICULATION :-

(a) Bilabial (=from/with two lips), i.e. the
consonant is produced with two lips

/p/   pack, pray, play, pull, part

happy, simple, spray, April,
apart

hope, tap, wrap, keep, stop

Note : 1. There is no system of making
the same consonant double in a word in
English. Whenever there are two
consonant letters together, the first one
becomes silent, e.g. the first "p" in
"happy".

2. Spellings in English are tricky.
It is because 44 speech sounds are
handled with only 26 letters of the
alphabet. Also, English has borrowed
many words from different languages.

Notice that '**w**' in the beginning of "**wrap**" is silent or mute.

/b/   back, buy, beast, because, best

labour, above, cubs, symbol, habit

tribe, rib, robe, club, job

/m/   man, mother, miss, much, most

games, lamp, image, America, among

lamb, room, game, him, team

/w/   where, want, within, watch, wait

sweet, swim, twelve, quite, quick

Note : 1. The sound /w/ cannot come at the end of a word in English.

2. The lips are rounded to produce /w/.

(b) Labio-dental (=from/with lip and teeth), i.e. the consonant is produced with the lower lip and the two front teeth.

/f/   fast, feel, fan, few, fail

afraid, difficult, office, before, often

cough, off, rough, life, laugh

/v/   very, veil, voice, view, value

over, river, seven, travel, heavy

of, twelve, move, believe, have

Note : The sound **/f/** is not there in Rajasthani or Hindi. Therefore, practise it carefully. The sound ^Q* is not the same as **/f/**.

(c) Dental (=from/with teeth), i.e. the consonant is produced with the tip of the tongue and the two front upper teeth.

/θ/   thick, three, thought, thirty, thirst

author, nothing, healthy, earthy, monthly

faith, fourth, month, south, death

/ð/   that, those, their, though, than

either, clothes, breathing, further,
worthy

bathe, smooth, clothe, breathe,
loathe

(d) Alveolar (=from with the teeth-ridge),
i.e. the consonant is articulated with the
tip &/or blade of the tongue against the
alveolar ridge.

/t/   two, town, Tuesday, talk, time

city, better, hotel, notice, watery

eight, but, great, missed, laughed

/d/   down, die, done, dinner,
December

idea, Monday, medicine, under,
ready

afraid, bad, friend, read, side

/n/   nice, notice, neither, need, know

many, winter, finish, final,
enough

green, join, rain, thirteen, begin

/s/   sink, said, south, sleep, start

beside, last, feast, listen,
message

face, cats, piece, advice, pass

/z/   zoo, Zed, zero, zinc, zone

lazy, busy, reason, noisy, losing,
miser

cause, noise, please, breeze, dogs

/l/   leaf, like, loud, learn, late

fellow, allow, foolish, believe,
feeling

tool, mile, fool, ball, owl

Note : The sound /z/ does not exist in Rajasthani or Hindi. Therefore, practise it well.

(e) Palato-alveolar (=from/with hard palate and alveolar ridge), i.e. the consonant is articulated with the tip/front of the tongue at the back of the alveolar ridge close to the hard palate. (Some phoneticians prefer to call them "post-alveolar" consonants.)

/ʃ/   shine, sure, should, sugar, sharp

machine, patient, nation, ashamed, anxious, ocean

push, selfish, punish, wash, fresh

/ʒ/   It does not begin any English word.

treasure, decision, pleasure, television, occasion

garage, rouge, beige, barrage

/tʃ/   change, chain, cheap, choice, child

teaching, kitchen, question, future, fortune

March, speech, stretch, which, touch

/dʒ/   joke, July, joy, journey, gentle

danger, soldier, subject, imagine, major

large, message, arrange, bridge,
page

/r/   read, round, write, rain, wrong

agree, cross, direct, foreign,
great

Note : 1. The sound /r/   does not
occur at the end of English words in R.P.
except when the following word begins
with a vowel (e.g. "never again'). Then it
is called the linking /r/.

2. The sound /ʒ/ is not there in
Rajasthani or Hindi. Therefore, make
enough practice to produce it correctly.

(f) Palatal (=from/with hard palate), i.e.
the consonant is produced with the tip and
blade of the tongue against the hard palate
as in /i:/ or / /.

/j/   yes, your, yellow, Europe, use

amuse, failure, few, knew, music

It does not occur at the end of
English words.

(g) Velar (=from/with velum or soft palate), i.e. the consonant is articulated with the back of the tongue and the soft palate.

/k/   class, kind, cool, kill, country

because, box, breakfast, pocket, school

lock, mistake, music, neck, break

/g/   gave, guard, garden, guess, green

ago, angry, August, forget, regular

bag, plug, drug, leg, dig

/ŋ/   It does not occur at the beginning of words in English.

singer, hungry, amongst, language, hanging

young, sing, wrong, spring, evening

(h) Glottal (=from/with glottis) i.e. the consonant is produced from the opening between the vocal cords.

/h/   heart, heat, haste, whose, how

behind, anyhow, key-hole,
inhale, greenhouse

It does not occur at the end of
English words.

(B) MANNER OF ARTICULATION
refers to the stricture involved in the
articulation of different consonants. The
term *'stricture'* means the way in which
the passage of air is restricted by the
various organs of speech. It is achieved
through two processes :-

**(i) 'Oro-Nasal Process' or 'Position of
the Velum':-** Speech sounds can be
classified as *'oral'* or *'nasal'*. This
depends upon the position of the velum or
soft-palate. If the soft palate (velum) is
raised, it makes a firm contact with the
back wall of the pharynx and shuts off the
nasal passage and allows the air to pass
through the oral passage. This is called
velic closure.

All the 20 vowels in English R.P. are articulated through the oral passage. Therefore, all the vowels are oral. In some languages, like French, Rajasthani and Hindi, there are nasalized vowels which are produced by allowing the air to pass through both the oral and the nasal passage. There are no such nasalized vowels in English. Out of the 24 English consonants, 21 consonants are articulated through the oral passage. They are called *'oral'* consonants.

If the air is blocked in the oral passage and allowed to pass through the nasal passage by keeping the soft palate lowered, *'nasal'* consonants are produced. There are only 3 *nasal* consonants, viz. /m/, /n/ and /ŋ/.

(ii)   Manipulation of Articulation :- Manipulating the different articulatory organs is the second process to achieve the desired stricture. Articulatory organs are divided into two groups of **(a)** Active Articulators and **(b)** Passive Articulators.

Active articulators make a movement during the production of speech sounds and **passive articulators** are those articulatory organs towards which the active articulators move. The lower lip and the tongue are active articulators. The upper lip and the entire roof of the mouth are passive articulators.

Having understood that we can now discuss the consonants on the basis of the manner of articulation :-

(a) Stop (or **Plosive**) **Consonants**
[complete closure & sudden release] :- The active articulator makes a firm contact with the passive articulator, and thus prevents the lung-air to escape through the mouth (**oral stop**). Simultaneously (=At the same time) there is a velic closure (**nasal stop**) so that the nasal passage is blocked. Thus, the lung-air gets compressed in the mouth. When the active articulator is suddenly removed from the passive articulator, the air comes out through the oral passage with a small **explosion** (burst). Therefore, *sounds articulated with a stricture of complete closure and sudden release are called* **plosives**. There are six such plosives in English. The initial sounds in the words

pin /p/, *bin* /b/ (bilabial), *tin* /t/, *din* /d/ (alveolar), *kin* /k/, and *gun* /g/ (velar) are plosives.

There are two types of stop : (i) oral stop and (ii) nasal stop. Therefore, when we talk about STOP consonants, we mean a complete stoppage of the airflow through both the nose and the mouth. For only oral stop without the nasal stop, the phoneticians use the term NASAL consonants. If the term *stop* appears confusing, the alternative *plosive* can be conveniently used without any confusion.

(b) Fricative Consonants [close approximation] :- The active articulator is brought so close to the passive articulator that there is a very narrow gap between them. The soft palate is raised so as to shut off the nasal passage. The lung-air is allowed to pass through the narrow space between the two articulators with slight **audible friction**. Such *sounds as are articulated with a stricture of close approximation are termed* **fricatives**. The initial sounds in the English words *fine, vine, thin, then, sip, zip, sheep* and *hat* as well as the final sound in *rouge* are fricatives. Thus, /f/, /v/ (labio-dental), /θ/, /ð/ (dental), /s/, /z/ (alveolar), /ʃ/, /ʒ/ (palato-alveolar), and /h/ (glottal)l are the nine fricatives in the R. P. Among these the four hissing sounds /s/, /z/,/ʃ/, and are /ʒ/ termed **sibilants**.

(c) Affricate [complete closure and slow release] :- These two sounds contain the qualities of both plosives and fricatives. The tip and blade of the tongue comes up to make contact with the back part of the alveolar ridge towards the hard palate to form an oral closure. The raised soft palate causes the velic nasal closure. The active articulator is removed slowly (*not suddenly*) from the passive articulator. Then, instead of the explosive noise (not like a plosive consonant), friction will be heard. This kind of combination of a plosive (complete closure) immediately followed by a fricative (slow release) is labelled **affricate**. The initial consonants in *cheap* /tʃ/ and *just* /dʒ/ (palato-alveolar) are **affricates**. Also, notice that only in the case of these two consonants there are two symbols each for a single sound. The first symbol represents a plosive and the second a fricative. These symbols also help us to understand that there is a combination of a plosive and a fricative in an affricate.

(d) Lateral [partial closure] :- The tongue-tip and the sides of the tongue-blade are in firm contact with the alveolar ridge. But the sides of the remainder of the tongue are not in contact with the sides of the palate. Thus, this stricture obstructs the airstream in the centre of the oral passage but allows it to pass through the gap between the sides of the tongue and the palate. The velic closure does not allow the air to pass through the nasal passage. *Sounds that are articulated with a stricture of complete closure in the centre of the vocal tract but with the air escaping along the sides of the tongue without any friction are called* **laterals**. The initial sound in the English word *love* /l/ (alveolar) is a lateral. This is the only lateral consonant in English.

(e) Gliding Consonants (or Approximants) [open approximation] :- There are three consonants which consist of a quick, smooth, non-friction glide towards a following vowel sound. For their articulation the soft palate is raised to shut off the nasal passage. The active articulator is brought close to the passive articulator so that the gap between them is wide (not *narrow* as in **fricatives**). The air escapes through this gap without friction. *Sounds that are articulated with a stricture of open approximation are called* **semi-vowels** [/j/ and /w/] and **frictionless continuants**. It was Peter Ladefoged (1975) who used the term **approximants** for the sounds that are articulated with a stricture of open approximation.

The initial sound in *yes* /j/ is a quick glide from the position of the vowel /iː/ or /ɪ/ (palatal) to the next vowel. Similarly, the initial sound in *weep* /w/ is a quick glide from the position of the vowel /uː/ or /ʊ/ (bilabial) to the next vowel. Because both the consonants begin from the position of a vowel (but they are consonants), they are called **semi-vowels**.

The initial sound /r/ in the word *read* is the third gliding consonant, but it does not resemble any English vowel like /j/ or /w/. The tongue has a curved shape with the tip pointing towards the hard palate at the back of the alveolar ridge (**post-alveolar**). The tongue-tip is not close enough to the palate to cause any friction. The soft palate is raised to close the nasal passage and the lung-air flows quietly between the tongue-tip and the palate without any friction. Therefore, this consonant is called **frictionless continuant**.

The letter '**r**' in English words like *red* and *ran* is pronounced as a **trill** by most Scottish people. **Trills** or **rolled consonants** are *sounds that are articulated with a stricture of intermittent closure*. To produce such a sound the soft palate is raised so that the nasal passage is shut off. Then the active articulator strikes against the passive articulator again and again. Thus, the air escapes between the two articulators intermittently. This is another variety of /r/ but not R.P.

There is yet another variety of the letter 'r' in the word *very*, which is pronounced as a **tap** or a **flap** by some English people. Again, this is not R.P. These varieties are well understood by the educated British speakers, but of course they sound foreign. In **taps** or **flaps** the active articulator strikes against the passive articulator just once (not several times as in **trills** or **rolled consonants**) and then quickly flaps forward.

Also, note that because there is no stoppage of air or friction in /l/, it is also included in the group of approximants and understood as **alveolar lateral approximant**. But it is usually called just **alveolar lateral** and its approximant status is assumed.

(f) Nasal [complete oral closure] :- There are three nasal sounds in English. They are the terminal sounds in *ram, ran* and *rang.* In their articulation, the stricture is like that of the plosives, i.e. the active and passive articulators are in firm contact with each other. Thus, they block off the oral passage of air completely. But, unlike the plosives, the soft palate is not raised (i.e. kept lowered) so that the nasal passage of air remains open. *Sounds that are articulated with a stricture of complete oral closure are called* **nasals**. Notice that the places of articulation of these nasals [/m/ (bilabial), /n/ (alveolar), /ŋ/ (velar)] are the same as that of the three pairs of plosives.

(C) STATE OF GLOTTIS (or **POSITION OF VOCAL CORDS**) is the third reference point to classify the consonants (or *to understand the difference between one consonant and another*). **Vocal cords** are a pair of lip-like structure in the larynx. They are positioned horizontally from front to back. They are attached at the front but can be separated at the back. The opening between the vocal cords is called the **glottis**. The **larynx** is also known as the

Adam's apple. It is situated at the top of the windpipe. The air from the lungs has to pass through the windpipe and the larynx during **exhaling** (or *expiration*).

The vocal cords can be opened and closed because they can be separated at the back. When these vocal cords come very close to each other, the glottis is shut completely. When we swallow food or water, the vocal cords shut the glottis so that food or water may not enter the windpipe.

Normally the vocal cords are drawn apart and the glottis is open so that we can breathe in and out without any difficulty. The air enters the lungs and comes out through the wide open glottis. Some consonant sounds are also produced in this **position of the vocal cords** (or the *state of the glottis*). Such sounds produced with a wide open glottis are called **voiceless** (or **breathed sounds** *because this is the position of the vocal cords while breathing*). The initial sound in *pin, tin, kin, fin, thin, sin, shin, hat,* and *chin* are the nine **voiceless consonants** in English. Remember that the first consonant of each of the pairs of **plosives** [bilabial /p/, alveolar /t/ & velar /k/], **fricatives** [labio-dental /f/, dental /θ/, alveolar /s/, palato-alveolar /ʃ/, & glottal /h/] and **affricates** [palato-alveolar /tʃ/] are **voiceless**. Voiceless glottal /h/ is a single consonant sound (i.e. without a pair) and has no **voiced** counterpart (or *partner*).

On the other hand, during the production of the remaining 15 consonants, the vocal cords are *loosely held together* (i.e. brought close to each other) and the pressure of the air from the lungs makes them open and close rapidly. This is called the vibration of the vocal cords. So the sounds articulated when the vocal cords vibrate are called **voiced**. All the consonant sounds in the words *bad, deal, girl, vine, then, zoo, measure, need, wing, red, yarn*, and *jug* are **voiced**. That is, /b/, /d/, /g/, /v/, /ð/, /z/, /ʒ/, /dʒ/, /l/, /j/, /w/, /r/, /m/, /n/, and /ŋ/ are the fifteen voiced consonants. Keep in mind that all vowel sounds are voiced. At the

time of whispering, all vowels and
consonants become voiceless. The
following figure will illustrate what we
have discussed:-

**Diagrams of the vocal cords : (a) tightly closed as for (?);
(b) wide open as for breath; (c) loosely together and vibrating as for voice.**

The vibration of the vocal cords is
important for another factor also. The
speed at which the vocal cords vibrate is
called the **frequency** (of vibration of the
vocal cords) and this determines the **pitch**
of the voice, which you will study about
later.

It is possible to feel the difference
between a voiceless and voiced sound.
We can use one of the two ways for that.
One, we can place our fingers lightly on
the Adam's apple during the production of
a certain sound. If the sound produced is
voiced, our fingers will feel the vibration
of the vocal cords. If the sound produced
is voiceless, our fingers will feel nothing.

For an example, if you produce a long *sssssssss* (i.e. a prolonged hissing sound) with your fingers on the Adam's apple, you do not feel any vibration. But, on the other hand, if you produce a long *zzzzzzz* (i.e. a prolonged buzzing sound), your fingers will feel the vibration. That proves that the sibilant /s/ is **voiceless** but the buzzing /z/ is **voiced**.

Some people think the second method easier. The same two sounds can be produced again with your palms placed gently on your ears. A buzz is heard when *zzzzzzz* is produced but no such buzz is heard in the case of *sssssssss*. These two ways can be repeated with other sounds like *fffffffff* and *vvvvvvvv*.

On the basis of the three terms discussed above we can very conveniently label and remember that :- /p/ is a

bilabial plosive voiceless   and /b/ is a

voiced bilabial plosive. Notice that there is no fixed rigid order for the three terms used. Anyone of them can precede or follow the other. These three terms can be used very conveniently to describe any consonant. Three terms are also used to label the vowel sounds of R.P. but they are different from the ones used here.

VOWELS : Unlike consonants, vowels are articulated with a stricture of open approximation That is, during the production of vowels there is **no obstruction** in the oral passage (as there is during *plosives*, *affricates*, *lateral*, and *nasals*) or **no friction** (as there is during *fricatives* or *affricates*). There is sufficient gap between the active and passive articulators to allow the lung-air to escape freely and continuously, **without any friction**.

The active articulator during the production of all vowels is (1) the **front** or (2) the **centre** or (3) the **back** of the tongue. The passive articulator is (a) the hard palate or (b) between back of hard palate and front of soft palate or (c) soft palate respectively. During the production of a vowel, the upper surface of the tongue is **convex** because some part of the tongue (front, central or back) is raised in the direction of the roof of the mouth.

There are 20 vowel sounds in English
(R.P.). Out of them 12 are called *pure
vowels* (or **monophthongs**) and 8 vowel
glides (or **diphthongs**). Thus, on the
basis of the part of the tongue that is
highest in the mouth during the
articulation of vowels, we can classify the
pure vowels (=monophthongs) of English
into three categories :-

(i) **Front vowels** (=during the articulation
of which the front of the tongue is raised
in the direction of the hard palate). The
vowels in the English words *bee* /iː/, *bid*
/ɪ/, *bed* /e/, and *bad* /æ/ are the *four* front
vowels.

(ii) **Back vowels** (=during the articulation
of which the back of the tongue is raised
in the direction of the soft palate). The
vowels in the English words *cart* /ɑː/, *cot*
/ɒ/, *caught* /ɔː/, *push* /ʊ/, and *pool* /uː/
are the **five** back vowels.

(iii) **Central vowels** (= during the
articulation of which the centre of the
tongue is raised in the direction of that
part of the roof of the mouth where the

hard palate and the soft palate meet). The underlined vowels in the English words *above* or *teacher* /ə/, *heard* /ɜː/ and *cup* /ʌ/ are the **three** central vowels.

However, all the four front vowels /iː/, /ɪ/, /e/, and /æ/ cannot be articulated in the same way. These vowels are produced by raising the front of tongue to different heights (or levels) with reference to the roof of the mouth. For producing /iː/ the tongue-front is the ***nearest*** to the hard palate and for /æ/ it is the ***farthest*** from the hard palate. Thus, on the basis of the height to which the tongue-part is raised, we can have four levels (or heights) of the part(s) of the tongue raised, viz.

(e) **Close** (or **High**) vowels (=during the articulation of which a specific part of the tongue is closest (=nearest) to the roof of the mouth. The vowels in the English words *beach* /iː/ and *boot* /uː/ are examples of close vowels.

(f)   **Open** (or **Low**) vowels (=during the articulation of which a specific part of the tongue is raised to a height farthest from the roof of the mouth). The vowels in the English words *part* /ɑ:/ and *pot* /ɒ/ are open vowels.

(g)   **Half-close** (or **Mid-high**) vowels are produced from a height between close and open positions, but nearer to **close** than to **open** position. The vowels in the English words *sit* /ɪ/ and *book* /ʊ/ are examples of half-close vowels.

(h)   **Half-open** (or **Mid-low**) vowels are produced from a height between close and open positions, but nearer to **open** than to **close**. The non-final vowel in the English word **s<u>u</u>bmit** /ə/ is a half-open vowel.

Keeping (1) the part of the tongue raised and (2) the height to which it is raised for the articulation of vowels we can have the following vowel-diagram (=chart). Remember that this quadrilateral refers to **cardinal vowels**. These cardinal vowels do not actually exist in any particular language of the world. These are only reference points which are used to study the vowels of various languages and not of English only. The area surrounded by the large quadrilateral is called the **vowel-area**, i.e. the area for the articulation of different vowel sounds of different languages.

The 12 pure vowels of English have been marked in the **Vowel-Diagram A**. The vowel-diagram gives us two criteria for the classification of vowels. Yet there is one more criterion, i.e. the position of lips. According to this, the vowels are divided into two categories:

(A) **Rounded vowels** (=during the articulation of which the lips are rounded. The vowels in the English words *shop* /ɒ/, *horse* /ɔː/, *pull* /ʊ/, and *cool* /uː/ are the four rounded vowels.

(B) **Unrounded vowels** (=during the production of which the lips are spread or neutral, but not rounded). The remaining eight monophthongs are unrounded.

To summarise, a vowel is studied through the following three criteria:-

(IV)   The part of the tongue raised during its articulation (front, central, back)

(V)   The height to which it is raised (close, half-close, half-open, open)

(VI)   The position of the lips (rounded, unrounded)

Now, we can take up the 12 pure vowels (monophthongs) one by one with its three-term labels and its occurrence in English words. Pay special attention to the spellings because different letters (or their combinations) give different sounds. This is the problem of the English language, which has to manage 44 sounds with 26 letters of the alphabet.

/iː/   front close unrounded

initially → eat, eel, eke, aegis

medially →beat, feel, geyser, seize, receive

terminally → bee, key, she, pea

/ɪ/front half-close unrounded

initially → it, if, in

medially → lid, rich, b<u>u</u>sy

terminally → cit<u>y</u>, recip<u>e</u>, sem<u>i</u>

/e/   **front unrounded between half-close and half-open**

initially → <u>a</u>ny, <u>e</u>nemy, <u>e</u>gg

medially →bed, pest, then

terminally → It does not occur finally in English words.

/æ/   **front unrounded just below half-open**

initially → axe, apple, ass

medially →bat, chap, hat

terminally → It does not occur terminally in English words.

/ɑː/   **back open unrounded vowel**

initially → <u>a</u>rt, <u>au</u>nt, <u>a</u>fter

medially →p<u>a</u>st, f<u>a</u>rm, cl<u>a</u>ss

finally → c<u>ar</u>, b<u>aa</u>, sp<u>a</u>

/ɒ/   **back rounded** (just above the)

open (position)

initially → <u>ho</u>nour, <u>o</u>ff, <u>o</u>ften

medially → sh<u>o</u>t, p<u>o</u>d, g<u>o</u>ne

terminally → It does not occur finally.

/ɔː/   **back rounded vowel between**

half-open and half-close

initially → <u>ou</u>ght, <u>a</u>ll, <u>Au</u>gust

medially → h<u>oa</u>rd, f<u>a</u>ll, f<u>ou</u>ght, f<u>au</u>lt

finally → l<u>aw</u>, m<u>ore</u>, f<u>our</u>

/ʊ/   **back rounded** (just above) **half-**

close

initially → It does not occur in the
beginning of English words, except
"*oomph*".

medially → p<u>u</u>t, s<u>u</u>gar, b<u>oo</u>k

terminally → Only in unaccented
(weak) preposition "*to*"

/uː/   **back close rounded** vowel

initially ➔ ooze, oodles

medially ➔ pool, shoed, boots

terminally ➔ zoo, shoe, to

/ɜː/   central unrounded vowel

between half-close & half-open

initially ➔ i̱rk, e̱arly, u̱rn

medially ➔ bu̱rn, fi̱rst, he̱ard

terminally ➔ monsi̱eur, messi̱eurs

/ə/   (when final) **central unrounded**

(just below) **half-open**

finally ➔ teacẖer, sof̱a, hoṉour

/ə/   (when non-final) **central**

unrounded between half-close & half-

open

[It is exactly like /ɜː/. The only

difference is that it is short.]

initially ➔ a̱bove, u̱tmost, a̱part

medially ➔ su̱bmit, pe̱rmit, co̱mpare

/ʌ/   **central unrounded** vowel

between half-open & open

initially → <u>u</u>nder, <u>u</u>p, <u>u</u>ncle

medially → cup, done, hunt

terminally → It does not occur.

Out of these 12 pure vowels, 5 are long while remaining 7 are short. The colon sign (:) after the symbols indicates length. Thus, the five vowels /iː/, /ɑː/, /ɔː/, /uː/, and /ɜː/ are long. Besides this length in general, every vowel (monophthong or diphthong) is relatively longer when it is <u>word-ending</u> or <u>followed by a voiced consonant</u> than <u>when it is followed by a voiceless consonant</u>. For example, /iː/ is longer in *'bee'* or *'beam'* than in *'beat'* and /aʊ/ is longer in *'bow'* or *'bowl'* than in *'bout'*. In a diphthong, it is the first element that is made long while the second element is very short.

Like monophthongs, 8 diphthongs have been shown in **Vowel-Diagram B** above. The dot shows the beginning and

the arrow indicates the direction of the
vowel glide. Notice that a diphthong is a
combination of two vowel sounds (as the
symbols suggest) but is considered to be a
single sound (phoneme). Diphthongs can
be put into 3 groups :- (i) ending in /ɪ/;

(ii) ending in /ʊ/; and (iii) ending in /ə/.

Let us take them up one by one.

/eɪ/   from **front unrounded just below half-**
close to **front unrounded** vowel **just**
above half-close

initially → eight, aim, age

medially → gate, straight, freight

terminally → pay, they, café

/aɪ/   from **front open unrounded** to
centralized front unrounded vowel just
above half-close

initially → ice, aisle, eyes

medially → price, type, sight, tied

terminally → pie, dye, cry

/ɔɪ/   from **back rounded vowel between open**

& half-open to **front unrounded vowel**

just above half-close

initially → oil, oyster

medially → choice, coin, foyer

terminally → boy, joy, annoy

/əʊ/   from **central unrounded vowel between**

half-close & half-open to **centralized**

back rounded vowel just above half-

close

initially → open, only, own, aubergine

medially → moan, quote, host,
chauffeur

terminally → go, foe, low, though

/aʊ/   from **back open unrounded** to

back half-close rounded

initially → owl, out, ouch

medially → fowl, bout, sound

terminally → how, cow, slough

/ɪə/   from centralized front unrounded

just above half-close to

**(3) central unrounded between half-close
& half-open** (if non-final)
(4) central unrounded just below half-open
(if final)

initially → ears, eerie

medially → merely, filial, union, beard,
fierce

terminally → here, sheer, fear, ar<u>ea</u>

/eə/   from **front half-open

unrounded** to

**(1) central unrounded between half-
close & half-open**, if non-final

**(2) central unrounded just below half-
open**, if final

initially → airy, area, aerodrome

medially → wary, shared, fairy, bears

terminally → hair, declare, there, tear

/ʊə/ from **centralized back rounded just above half-close** to

(1) central unrounded between half-close & half-open, if non-final

(2) central unrounded just below half-open, if final

initially → It does not occur.

medially → purely, Europe, gourd

terminally → poor, sure, you're, bluer

Earlier we studied that half of our body is involved during speech and that many organs are used to produce different sounds. But we had a mere reference to these *organs of speech* divided into three groups of respiratory, phonatory and articulatory systems. We can now study them in a slightly detailed manner but we shall go in the order of the above-mentioned three groups. But before that look at the **figure** below, which shows different parts used in the articulation of speech sounds. [LL=lips; TT= Teeth; TR=Teeth Ridge; HP= Hard Palate; SP = Soft Palate; Bl=Blade of the tongue;

F=Front of the tongue; B= Back of the
tongue; R= Root of the tongue; U=
Uvula; P= Pharynx; E= Epiglottis; V=
Vocal cords; W=Windpipe; P= Food
Pipe]

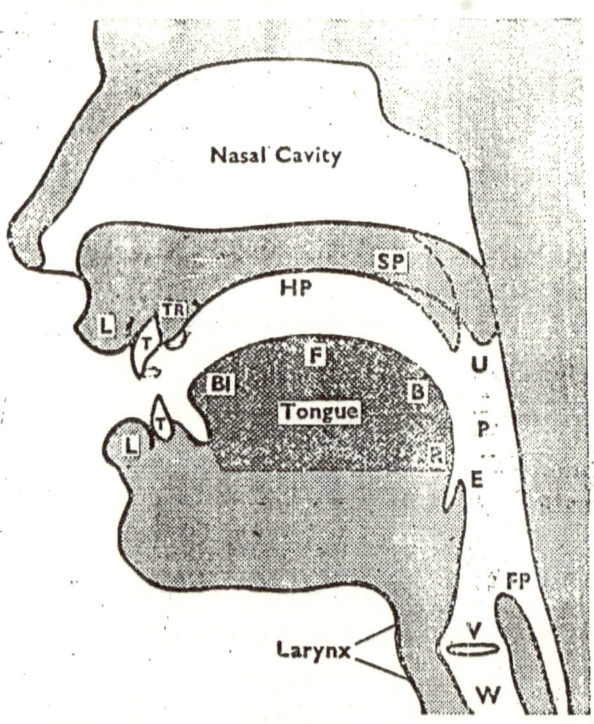

1. Respiratory system is mainly used
for breathing but it is also used for
speaking. For speech production we need
an air-stream. The air going out of the

lungs provides energy for producing various speech sounds. This system involves the lungs, the chest muscles, the windpipe, the pharynx, and the nose. Here two things need to be noted. First, that an organ belonging to one system, e.g. the nose, can be repeated in another system, e.g. the articulatory system, also. Secondly, some organs help directly, and some indirectly, in the production of speech.

The **lungs** are a pair of spongy balloon-like bodies. They are made of small sacs called the **alveoli** (singular *'alveolus'*). In these sacs, blood is cleaned of its carbon-dioxide and provided with fresh oxygen from the outer air. Air is supplied to the alveoli by small tubes called the **bronchioles**. The bronchioles come together into two large tubes called the **bronchi** (singular *'bronchus'*), one on the right and the other on the left. Each bronchus joins the **windpipe** (or *'trachea'*) to the lungs. It is through the windpipe that the air we breathe in passes through the throat into the lungs. The windpipe is in front of the food-pipe (oesophagus). The act of respiration (breathing) involves two processes— taking outer air into (*breathing in*) the lungs [called 'inspiration' or 'inhalation'] and throwing out air *(breathing out)* from the lungs into the atmosphere [called 'expiration' or 'exhalation']. It is the expiratory lung-air that is used for the articulation of most speech sounds of all languages. It provides the energy needed for the articulation of speech sounds. You must have realised that when this energy is exhausted while speaking, we have to stop in order to breathe in and out to speak again. This air-stream involving lung-air is called **pulmonic air-stream**.

The pulmonic air-stream mechanism consists of the lungs and the respiratory muscles (chest muscles). The walls of the lungs are moved by the

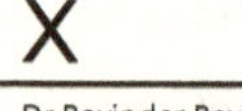

respirat ory muscles so that the air is drawn into the lungs or pushed out of them. When this air-stream mechanism is used to push

air out, it is called *egressive*; and when it
is used to draw air in, it is termed
ingressive.

As mentioned earlier, most speech
sounds make use of **pulmonic egressive**
air-stream mechanism. In fact, all the
sounds of English are produced with this
air-stream mechanism. It is possible to
articulate speech sounds using **pulmonic
ingressive** air-stream mechanism, but no
language uses it. It is used for yawning
and snoring, but not for speaking.

2. Phonatory system is responsible
for supplying the musical note or *'voice'*
to the speech sound. On the basis of the
presence of 'voice', some sounds are
called 'voiced'. Those sounds are called
'voiceless' whose articulation is without
'voice'. This system comprises the larynx
and the vocal folds (or ***cords***) inside it.
You have already read that during
whispering, all sounds become voiceless.
Therefore, it is not possible to sing in the
whispering mode because no musical
notes can be added to the singer's voice.

Larynx is the upper part of the windpipe where the vocal cords are found. It is perceived as the most important part of the mechanism of speech production, because it is the generator (source) of speech sounds, particularly the voiced sounds produced by the vibration of the vocal cords. The air released from the lungs comes up through the windpipe and arrives first at the larynx, which is the independent producer of <u>voice</u>, i.e. voiced sounds. The larynx contains two small bands of elastic tissues, which can be thought of as two flat strips of rubber lying opposite each other across the air passage. These are the ***vocal cords*** or ***vocal folds***. They are positioned horizontally from front to back. The vocal cords are attached at the front but can be separated at the back. The inner edges of the vocal cords can be moved towards each other so that they meet and completely cover the top of the windpipe; or they can be held apart so that there is a gap between them, known as the *glottis*, through which the air can pass freely. This is the usual position of the vocal cords when we breathe quietly in and out. Figure 2 clearly indicates the various parts of the phonatory system.

When the vocal cords are brought together tightly, no air can pass through them and if the lungs are pushing air from below, this air gets compressed. If the vocal cords are then opened suddenly, the compressed air bursts out with a sort of coughing noise. Such holding back of the compressed air followed by a sudden release is called the glottal stop; and what we feel as the air bursts out is the vocal cords springing apart.

However, if the vocal cords are brought together quite gently, the air from the lungs will be able to force them apart for a moment, but then they will return to the closed position again; then the air will force them apart again, and they will close again, and so on. This is a very rapid process and averages 125 times per second in male voices, 210 times per second in female voices and over 300 in children's voices. Obviously, it is not possible to hear each individual 'click' of the opening and closing of vocal cords. What we actually hear is a musical note.

The note, whether high or low, produced by this rapid opening and closing of vocal cords is called '**voice**'. Some of the English sounds that have voice are called '*voiced*'. All the vowel sounds are voiced and 15 consonants are also voiced. The sounds which are not voiced are called '*voiceless*'; and are produced with the vocal cords drawn apart so that the air can pass out freely between them without vibration. 9 consonants are voiceless. The difference between voiced and voiceless is important to distinguish between what are otherwise similar sounds, e.g. voiced /z/ and voiceless /s/. All this and a few other things related with the phonatory system have already been discussed under the heading "STATE OF GLOTTIS or POSITION OF VOCAL CORDS". Read that again for better understanding of the system.

3. Articulatory system is the system which is chiefly related with the articulation of speech sounds. The organs of speech above the larynx are called **articulators**. On that score, we can term the organs of respiratory system as '**respirators**' and those of phonatory system as '**phonators**'.

The passage of air above the larynx is known as the '**vocal tract**'. From the uvula this vocal tract gets divided into (a) '**oral tract**' below the uvula extending to the lips; and (b) '**nasal tract**' above the uvula extending to the nose. Raising or lowering the velum (called '*oro-nasal process*') controls the oral and nasal tracts to produce oral and nasal sounds.

We have already discussed the difference between the *active* articulators and *passive* articulators. You will realise that the *lower* articulators are active and *upper* articulators are passive. The articulators can also be divided into further two groups of *movable* and immovable. Now we can discuss these articulators one by one.

(a) **Pharynx** is the cavity at the top of the throat which connects nasal and oral passages on one side and oesophagus (food-pipe) and larynx on the other side. In other words, it is the hollow area just above the larynx up to the entrance of the oral or nasal cavities. It is about 8 centimetres in men and 7 centimetres in women. At the top end it is divided into two parts : one being the back of the mouth and the other beginning of the way to the nasal cavity.

(b) **Soft Palate** (or **Velum**) is a muscular flap that can be raised to press against the back wall of the pharynx and shut off the nasal tract, thus preventing air from going out through the nose. This action is called *velic closure*. It separates the nasal tract from the oral tract so that the air can pass only through the mouth. At the lower end of the velum is a small appendage hanging down, called the uvula. The part of the vocal tract between the uvula and the larynx is the pharynx. Thus, the back wall of the pharynx may be considered to be one of the articulators on the upper surface of the vocal tract. The velum is an articulator in two ways : (i) when it is raised, the airstream coming from the lungs through the larynx cannot escape through the nose; (ii) it can be touched by the tongue to produce certain sounds. To produce the sounds /k/, / /

and / / the back of the tongue is in contact with the lower side of the velum. Therefore, we call these sounds <u>velar sounds</u> or <u>velar consonants</u>.

(c) **Hard Palate** (or **Palate)** : The palate forms the roof of the mouth and separates the mouth/oral cavity from the nose/nasal cavity. When we make the tip of the tongue touch as much of our palate as we can, we feel that most of it is hard and fixed. But when the tongue-tip goes as far back as it can go, away from the teeth, we notice that the palate becomes soft. The hard fixed part of the palate is divided into two sections : the <u>alveolar/teeth ridge</u> and the <u>hard palate</u>. The hard palate is the highest part of the palate between the alveolar ridge and the beginning of the velum. The hard palate, curving downwards towards the teeth at each side, is the front part of the mouth formed by a bony structure. During the articulation of the semi-vowel /j/, the front of the tongue comes close to the hard palate, allowing a gap to produce sound without any friction. Therefore, this sound is called <u>palatal</u>. Because the soft palate is called <u>velum</u>, the hard palate can simply be called the <u>palate</u> without any confusion.

(d) **Alveolar Ridge** (or **Teeth Ridge** or **Alveolum**) : Just behind the upper teeth there is a small protuberance that can be felt with the tip of the tongue. This is covered with little ridges. It is called the alveolar/teeth ridge and is specially important in English because many of the consonants like /t/, /d/, /n/, /l/, /r/, /s/, /z/, / /, / /, /t /, /d / are produced with the tongue touching or being close to the alveolar ridge.

(e) **Tongue** is the most important articulatory organ because it has the greatest variety of movements. Although it has no natural divisions like the palate, it is convenient to think of it as divided into five parts. The <u>tip and blade</u> of the tongue are the most mobile parts. The tip and the blade lie under the alveolar ridge—the tip being the most forward part of all and the blade between the tip and the front of the tongue. Behind the blade lies what is technically called the <u>front</u> of the tongue : it is actually the forward part of the tongue and lies underneath the hard palate when the tongue is at rest. The remainder of the tongue can be divided into the <u>centre</u> (which is partly beneath the hard palate and partly beneath the velum), the <u>back</u> (which is beneath the soft palate when the tongue is at rest) and the <u>root</u> (which is opposite the back wall of the pharynx). The epiglottis is attached to the lower part of the root of the tongue. Because of this mobile and elastic nature of the tongue, it is very important in producing many consonants and vowels as well.

(f) Teeth : The lower front teeth are not important in speech production except that if they are missing, certain sounds (e.g. /s/ and /z/) will be difficult to articulate. But the two upper front teeth are used in English. When we put the tip of the tongue very close to the edge of these teeth and blow, it will produce a sound like / / as in the English word *thin*. If we turn on the voice *(by bringing the vocal cords closer to produce voiced sounds)* during this / / sound, we shall get a sound like / / as in the English word *then*. Such sounds, made with the tongue touching the front upper teeth are called <u>dental</u>.

(g) Lips are obviously important in speech since they can take up various shapes : (1) they can be pressed together firmly to block the air passage through the mouth to produce sounds like /p/, /b/ and /m/; (2) the lower lip can be drawn inward and moved slightly upward to bring in contact with the upper front teeth to articulate the sounds /f/ and /v/; (3) they can be rounded with different amounts as in /u:/, / / or /w/; (4) they can be kept apart in flat unrounded positions as in /e/ or / /; (5) they can be spread as in /i:/; or (6) they can be pushed forward to a greater or lesser extent for certain sounds. Sounds like /p/, /b/, /m/, or /w/, in which both lips are in contact with each other or rounded, are technically called <u>bilabial</u>.

The seven articulators described above are the major articulators used in the production of speech sounds, yet there are three marginal ones which can be considered articulators because they are essential for making certain types of sounds.

(h) **Jaws** are not directly involved in the articulation of sounds but they, too, are active and operative in order to give different shapes needed to produce various sounds.

(i) **Nose** has already been mentioned in the respiratory system because it is mainly used for breathing. However, the nasal cavity is very important while articulating *nasal* sounds, e.g. /m/, /n/ and / / in English. For producing a nasal consonant, the air is prevented from going out through the mouth, e.g. by closing the two lips for /m/. Because the soft palate is kept lowered, the air can pass through the nose to make a nasal sound. For oral sounds the velum is raised to block the nasal passage, known as the *velic closure.* Also, in some languages, like Hindi and French, the vowels are nasalized by allowing the air to go out through both the mouth and the nose.

(j) The importance of the **EAR** in checking, controlling and correcting our own speech was explained in the handout titled 'Phonetics–I'. We are not going to repeat it. Nevertheless, the main value of the ear in relation to the listener is the field of 'Auditory Phonetics', which you will study later.

Thus, we have learnt the significance of the various organs in producing the sounds of a language, which comes under 'Articulatory Phonetics'. The following brief descriptions of a few organs already mentioned will also be helpful.

Windpipe : It is the passage of air from lungs to the throat. Technically it is known as '*trachea*'.

Epiglottis : It is the small flat part at the root of the tongue, which is lowered during swallowing to prevent food, etc. from entering the windpipe.

Uvula : It is a small piece of fleshy matter dangling/hanging from the back of the velum.

Oesophagus : It is the tube at the bottom of pharynx which takes food to the stomach.